From Rome to Kampala

The U.S. Approach to
the 2010 International Criminal Court
Review Conference

COUNCIL *on*
FOREIGN
RELATIONS

Council Special Report No. 55
April 2010

Vijay Padmanabhan

From Rome to Kampala
The U.S. Approach to
the 2010 International Criminal Court
Review Conference

The Council on Foreign Relations is an independent, nonpartisan membership organization, think tank, and publisher dedicated to being a resource for its members, government officials, business executives, journalists, educators and students, civic and religious leaders, and other interested citizens in order to help them better understand the world and the foreign policy choices facing the United States and other countries. Founded in 1921, the Council carries out its mission by maintaining a diverse membership, with special programs to promote interest and develop expertise in the next generation of foreign policy leaders; convening meetings at its headquarters in New York and in Washington, DC, and other cities where senior government officials, members of Congress, global leaders, and prominent thinkers come together with Council members to discuss and debate major international issues; supporting a Studies Program that fosters independent research, enabling Council scholars to produce articles, reports, and books and hold roundtables that analyze foreign policy issues and make concrete policy recommendations; publishing *Foreign Affairs*, the preeminent journal on international affairs and U.S. foreign policy; sponsoring Independent Task Forces that produce reports with both findings and policy prescriptions on the most important foreign policy topics; and providing up-to-date information and analysis about world events and American foreign policy on its website, CFR.org.

The Council on Foreign Relations takes no institutional positions on policy issues and has no affiliation with the U.S. government. All statements of fact and expressions of opinion contained in its publications are the sole responsibility of the author or authors.

Council Special Reports (CSRs) are concise policy briefs, produced to provide a rapid response to a developing crisis or contribute to the public's understanding of current policy dilemmas. CSRs are written by individual authors—who may be CFR fellows or acknowledged experts from outside the institution—in consultation with an advisory committee, and are intended to take sixty days from inception to publication. The committee serves as a sounding board and provides feedback on a draft report. It usually meets twice—once before a draft is written and once again when there is a draft for review; however, advisory committee members, unlike Task Force members, are not asked to sign off on the report or to otherwise endorse it. Once published, CSRs are posted on www.cfr.org.

For further information about CFR or this Special Report, please write to the Council on Foreign Relations, 58 East 68th Street, New York, NY 10065, or call the Communications office at 212.434.9888. Visit our website, www.cfr.org.

To submit a letter in response to a Council Special Report for publication on our website, CFR.org, you may send an email to CSReditor@cfr.org. Alternatively, letters may be mailed to us at: Publications Department, Council on Foreign Relations, 58 East 68th Street, New York, NY 10065. Letters should include the writer's name, postal address, and daytime phone number. Letters may be edited for length and clarity, and may be published online. Please do not send attachments. All letters become the property of the Council on Foreign Relations and will not be returned. We regret that, owing to the volume of correspondence, we cannot respond to every letter.

This report is printed on paper that is certified by SmartWood to the standards of the Forest Stewardship Council, which promotes environmentally responsible, socially beneficial, and economically viable management of the world's forests.

Mixed Sources
Product group from well-managed forests and other controlled sources
www.fsc.org   Cert no. SW-COC-001530
© 1996 Forest Stewardship Council
FSC

Contents

Foreword

The United States has long been a leading force behind international efforts to bring the perpetrators of atrocities to justice. It spearheaded the prosecution of German and Japanese officials after World War II and more recently supported tribunals to deal with events in Rwanda, the former Yugoslavia, and elsewhere. Washington has kept far more distance, however, from the International Criminal Court (ICC). Although President Bill Clinton allowed U.S. negotiators to sign the Rome Statute, the agreement that established the court, he and subsequent presidents have maintained objections to elements of the court's jurisdiction and prosecutorial authority. U.S. administrations have since cooperated to varying degrees with the ICC, but the notion of ratifying the Rome Statute and joining the court has never been seriously entertained.

Even as a nonmember, though, the United States has important interests at stake in the ICC's operations. On the one hand, the court can bring to justice those responsible for atrocities, something with both moral and strategic benefits. On the other hand, there are fears that the court could seek to investigate American actions and prosecute American citizens, as well as concerns that it will weaken the role of the UN Security Council (where the United States has a veto) as the preeminent arbiter of international peace and security.

This Council Special Report, authored by Vijay Padmanabhan, examines how the United States should advance its interests at the ICC's 2010 review conference, scheduled for May and June in Kampala, Uganda. After outlining the history of U.S. policy toward the court, the report analyzes the principal items on the review conference agenda, most notably the debate over the crime of aggression. The conference faces the task of deciding whether to adopt a definition of aggression and, should it do so, whether and how to activate the court's jurisdiction over this crime. Padmanabhan explains the important questions this debate raises.

Offering guidance for U.S. policy, the report recommends that the United States not seek to join the court in the foreseeable future. However, Padmanabhan urges the Obama administration to make an active case for its preferred outcomes at the review conference, including by sending a cabinet-level official to Kampala. On the question of aggression, he calls for a strong stand against activating the ICC's jurisdiction. He argues that the proposed definition is overly vague, something that could endanger U.S. interests and risk embroiling the court in political disputes over investigations. Should the review conference nonetheless adopt a definition, he advises the administration to emphasize the potential drawbacks of activating the ICC's jurisdiction without consensus among its members. On other issues, the report urges the United States to contribute constructively to the evaluation of the court's functioning that the conference will carry out. And if the conference's overall outcome is favorable, Padmanabhan concludes, the United States should consider boosting its cooperation with the court in such areas as training, funding, the sharing of intelligence and evidence, and the apprehension of suspects.

From Rome to Kampala offers a timely agenda for U.S. policy at this year's review conference and toward the ICC in general. Its thoughtful analysis and detailed recommendations make an important addition to current thinking on a set of issues with deep moral, legal, and strategic implications.

Richard N. Haass
President
Council on Foreign Relations
April 2010

Acknowledgments

I would like to thank this report's advisory committee for their timely and incisive advice, suggestions, and support. While I understand that several committee members do not agree with this report's approach or recommendations, their contributions were nonetheless extremely valuable. I am grateful to CFR President Richard N. Haass and Director of Studies James M. Lindsay, the publishing department's Patricia Dorff and Lia Norton, and Research Associate Gideon Copple. I would also like to thank Cathy Adams, Stefan Barriga, Todd Buchwald, John Daley, Arto Haapea, Matthew Heaphy, Karen H. Johnson, Mike Mattler, and William L. Nash, whose time and experience were essential to the completion of this report.

The John D. and Catherine T. MacArthur Foundation supported this project as part of its broader grant to the CFR Program on International Justice, and its generosity is appreciated. This report was prepared with the guidance of Program on International Justice codirectors John B. Bellinger III and Matthew C. Waxman, whose tireless efforts are reflected in the final report. Also special thanks to Walter B. Slocombe for chairing the advisory committee and providing thoughtful guidance throughout the drafting process.

Although many have contributed to this endeavor from conception to publication, the findings and recommendations herein are solely my own, and I accept full responsibility for them.

Vijay Padmanabhan

Council Special Report

Introduction

For the foreseeable future the United States is unlikely to become a member of the International Criminal Court (ICC), the international tribunal in The Hague responsible for prosecuting human rights atrocities and war crimes. From the time the Rome Statute of the International Criminal Court (the "Rome Statute")—the treaty that established the ICC—was negotiated in 1998, the United States has voiced strong concerns about the ICC exercising jurisdiction over nationals of nonparties and the ICC prosecutor's authority to investigate and prosecute suspects without the approval of the UN Security Council. Those concerns have not been alleviated, and the Obama administration has said that it will not seek U.S. Senate approval of the Rome Statute in the near future. Even if the treaty were submitted to the Senate, the Senate would not approve it in its current form. Moreover, U.S. concerns could be exacerbated by modifications to the Rome Statute ICC members may make in the coming months.

While remaining outside the Rome Statute, the United States nevertheless shares with the ICC a commitment to prosecute perpetrators of genocide, crimes against humanity, and serious war crimes (collectively known as "atrocity crimes"). The United States has historically been the leader in international justice efforts both for moral reasons and because those crimes undermine peace and respect for rule of law. Widespread support for the court among other states means it has become and will remain the presumptive forum for future international trials of the worst perpetrators of war crimes and mass atrocities.

The United States has struggled to balance its support for the ICC's aims with its underlying concerns about the institution. The early years of the Bush administration were marked by strong opposition to the court, but this position shifted during the second Bush term and under the Obama administration to a cautious willingness to support the ICC where consonant with U.S. interests.

At the end of May 2010, the parties to the Rome Statute will hold a review conference in Kampala, Uganda, that will test the new relationship between the ICC and the United States. Given the importance of the review conference, the Obama administration has decided that the United States will attend the Kampala Conference as an observer, and it is currently considering its negotiating strategy. A lesson learned from U.S. participation in the Rome Conference that drafted the Rome Statute was that going in without a clear and carefully considered strategy severely limited U.S. influence during the treaty negotiations. The Obama administration should therefore act quickly to solidify its negotiating position before the review conference.

The review conference will consider amendments to the Rome Statute, including whether to authorize the court to prosecute the crime of "aggression," an offense over which the ICC has jurisdiction but which was left undefined in the Rome Statute. As the United States takes cautious steps toward the ICC, adding aggression to the court's jurisdiction could widen the distance between the United States and the ICC, perhaps irreversibly. The primary U.S. objective for Kampala therefore should be to dissuade state parties from activating the court's jurisdiction over aggression in a manner that undermines the potentially valuable work of the ICC in prosecuting atrocity crimes, as well as the security interests of the United States.

Prosecuting aggression risks miring the court in political disputes regarding the causes of international controversies, thereby diminishing its effectiveness and perceived legitimacy in dispensing justice for atrocity crimes. ICC jurisdiction over aggression also poses unique risks to the United States as a global superpower. It places U.S. and allied leaders at risk of prosecution for what they view as necessary and legitimate security actions. Adding aggression to the ICC's mandate would also erode the primacy of the UN Security Council in managing threats to international peace. For these reasons, a decision among state parties in Kampala to add aggression crimes to the ICC's jurisdiction would jeopardize U.S. cooperation with the court, including possible future financial and infrastructure assistance, political and military support in capturing suspects, and classified information sharing essential to prosecutions. The ICC will be more successful with such assistance.

In addition to aggression, the review conference will also assess the performance of the ICC since it began operations in 2002. The United States should seize the opportunity to emphasize specific ways to improve the court's effectiveness in holding perpetrators of atrocity crimes accountable. This will allow the United States to have greater influence with ICC parties and assert more strongly its leadership in seeking justice for the worst perpetrators of atrocities.[1]

Achieving U.S. objectives at Kampala will not be easy. Although many ICC parties are pleased to see the Obama administration engaging more actively with the court, the United States will be present at the review conference only as an observer state with no immediate plans to ratify the Rome Statute and become a state party. The absence of the United States from ICC institutions during the Bush administration may fuel resentment toward active U.S. involvement at the review conference if U.S. positions are seen as obstructionist. Other states at the conference may also view U.S. positions on international justice issues suspiciously in the aftermath of the invasion of Iraq, and because of the perception that the United States has failed to hold officials accountable for detainee abuse. Meanwhile, in the United States, opposition to or skepticism about the ICC within the Pentagon and Congress will limit the Obama administration's ability to make substantial offers of support to the court, especially during an election year.

Nevertheless, given its role as a global superpower and involvement in the long-term success of the ICC, the United States has the opportunity to secure an outcome from the review conference that will further U.S. foreign policy interests. If U.S. concerns could be addressed at some future point through changes to the Rome Statute, it would be desirable for the United States to become a member of the court. But because U.S. concerns about the ICC are bipartisan and reflect the unique role and interests of the United States as a global military power and permanent UN Security Council member, it is unlikely that they will be sufficiently alleviated in the foreseeable future to make it wise or politically possible for the United States to join the court. Instead, U.S. policy should focus on increasing cooperation with the court where U.S. and ICC interests align, while continuing to seek ways to protect U.S. security interests. In that vein, if the United States is able to achieve its objectives in Kampala, it should consider formalizing a working relationship with the ICC as a "nonparty partner" through a U.S. agreement to support aspects of the court's work.

The Road to Now:
The United States and the ICC

The United States has historically been at the forefront of efforts to create international institutions to prosecute atrocity crimes. After World War II, the United States led Allied efforts to prosecute top German and Japanese officials for atrocity crimes and crimes against the peace (aggression), overcoming British and Soviet arguments for summary execution of the enemy leadership.

During the Clinton administration, the United States provided the political impetus behind the Security Council's creation of international tribunals to prosecute those who committed atrocity crimes in Rwanda and the former Yugoslavia. The United States was instrumental in funding and staffing the tribunals, as well as in prodding states to cooperate with them. These tribunals ushered in an era of special-purpose ad hoc international tribunals for Sierra Leone, Cambodia, and Lebanon that were endorsed by the Security Council and supported by the United States.

The enormous cost and time-lag difficulties involved in creating ad hoc tribunals led the UN General Assembly to convene a conference in Rome in 1998 for the purpose of establishing a permanent international criminal court. The resulting Rome Statute grants the ICC jurisdiction over atrocity crimes. It also grants the ICC jurisdiction over the crime of aggression, but only once a provision is adopted "defining the crime and setting out the conditions under which the court shall exercise jurisdiction." The U.S. delegation made serious efforts in advance of and during the Rome Conference to establish a court that would prosecute, at the request of the Security Council, those responsible for atrocity crimes that national courts are unable or unwilling to prosecute. U.S. efforts were instrumental in ensuring that the ICC is used today only as a last resort, and only to address the most serious atrocity crimes. The principle that the ICC prosecutes crimes only where national courts with jurisdiction cannot or will not act is known as "complementarity," and it remains an important tenet in guiding the court's actions.

Nevertheless, the United States was one of only seven states to vote against the final Rome Statute.[2] The United States had two main objections. First, the text granted the ICC jurisdiction over crimes committed by nationals of states that are not parties to the Rome Statute if the crimes occur in the territory of a state party. This provision potentially exposes U.S. military personnel involved in peacekeeping and other security operations to the risk of ICC prosecution, regardless of whether the United States joins the court.

Second, the Rome Statute created a self-initiating prosecutor empowered to proceed with prosecutions without the consent of the Security Council.[3] Although the Rome Statute grants the Security Council authority to delay investigations or prosecutions for up to a year, it rejected proposals by the five permanent Security Council members (P5) that conditioned jurisdiction on Security Council referral. The United States argued that this structure was inconsistent with the UN Charter, which grants the Security Council primary authority in maintaining international peace and security.

The Clinton administration continued to participate in ICC meetings despite its vote at Rome. President Bill Clinton authorized U.S. negotiators to sign the Rome Statute on December 31, 2000, the last possible day for signature. One hundred thirty-nine states, including all of the P5 states except for China, signed the Rome Statute, but not all of them have ratified or formally become parties to it. President Clinton argued that the signature enhanced U.S. capacity to shape future developments at the ICC. But in a signing statement, Clinton added that he was recommending president-elect George W. Bush not submit the treaty to the Senate for advice and consent until U.S. concerns were addressed.

Upon taking office, President Bush took active steps to distance the United States from the ICC. The ICC became operational on July 1, 2002, when the Rome Statute came into effect. In advance of that event, the United States sent a letter to the United Nations, signed by then undersecretary of state John R. Bolton, stating that the United States did not intend to become a party to the Rome Statute.[4] Undersecretary of State for Political Affairs Marc Grossman explained that the letter was designed to release the United States from the international legal obligation created upon the Clinton administration's signature to act consistently with the "object and purpose" of the Rome Statute. Nevertheless, Grossman identified "common ground" between the United States and ICC state parties, and "ask[ed] those nations who have decided to join the Rome Treaty to meet us there."[5]

Later in 2002, Congress passed and President Bush signed the American Service-Members' Protection Act (ASPA). ASPA prohibited sharing classified information and other forms of cooperation with the ICC, restricted aid to state parties that did not complete bilateral non-surrender agreements (also called Article 98 agreements), shielding U.S. forces from ICC jurisdiction, and authorized the president to use "all means necessary" to secure the release of U.S. or allied officials detained at the ICC's request. Consistent with ASPA, the United States began blocking reauthorization of UN peacekeeping missions whose mandates did not guarantee immunity for U.S. forces from ICC jurisdiction. The United States also negotiated more than one hundred bilateral non-surrender agreements prohibiting transfer of American citizens to the ICC. All of these steps were widely perceived by ICC parties as part of a strategy by the Bush administration to undermine the fledgling court.

U.S. policy toward the ICC began to shift in President Bush's second term, as State and Defense department officials recognized that some of these actions were undermining U.S. foreign policy interests, including important military relationships, and that the ICC served U.S. interests in certain situations. The State Department legal adviser explained in a series of speeches that the Bush administration sought a "modus vivendi" with the ICC based on mutual respect.[6] The United States was now willing to work with the ICC where they shared goals related to international justice. In return, the United States requested that the international community respect its decision not to become party to the ICC.

This new U.S. attitude manifested itself in two concrete ways. First, President Bush issued a series of waivers to the statutory funding cutoffs, and in 2008 Congress repealed restrictions on provision of military aid to state parties. This shift on funding led the United States to abandon further efforts to secure bilateral non-surrender agreements.

Second, the United States cooperated with the ICC on Sudan and Sierra Leone. The United States abstained on UN Security Council Resolution 1593, which referred the Darfur situation to the ICC.

Following that referral, the United States was a strong supporter of the ICC's efforts in Sudan, offering assistance to the prosecutor and blocking efforts by African and Islamic states to delay investigations through the Security Council. The United States also agreed to allow the Special Court for Sierra Leone to use the ICC facilities in The Hague for the prosecution of former Liberian president Charles Taylor.

Upon assuming office in January 2009, the Obama administration immediately began a review of U.S. policy toward the ICC. Although elements of this review continue, Ambassador-at-Large for War Crimes Issues Stephen J. Rapp stated publicly that the Obama administration does not expect to present the Rome Statute to the Senate for advice and consent in the near future. Nevertheless, the United States began participating in the ICC's Assembly of States Parties in November 2009, and the Obama administration has committed to attending the Kampala Review Conference as an observer. The Obama administration explained this decision as a way to express directly to ICC parties U.S. concerns regarding activation of the ICC's jurisdiction over aggression.[7] The Obama administration has also continued cooperation with active ICC investigations, recently announcing it would assist in providing security to witnesses in Kenya who provide testimony to the ICC.

THE ICC TODAY

Today III states have ratified and become parties to the Rome Statute, including all members of the European Union, Australia, Canada, Japan, and most of Latin America and Africa. In addition to the United States, nonparties include China, Russia, India, Iraq, and Israel.

The ICC has exercised jurisdiction in five situations to date. In three of these situations—Uganda, the Democratic Republic of the Congo (DRC), and the Central African Republic—the state itself referred the case to the ICC. In Darfur, Sudan, the Security Council referred the case to the ICC prosecutor, Luis Moreno-Ocampo, for investigation. In Kenya, the prosecutor opened a formal investigation into postelection violence on his own initiative.

To date, the ICC has eight pending warrants for arrest and four defendants in custody awaiting trial. One other suspect, Sudanese rebel leader Bahr Idriss Abu Garda, has voluntarily appeared in front of the

ICC, but is not under arrest. The first trial at the ICC began in January 2009. Thomas Lubanga Dyilo, a Congolese warlord, is alleged to have recruited and deployed children in armed conflict. A second trial against two other Congolese warlords is also under way. The ICC's third trial, against former DRC vice president Jean-Pierre Bemba Gombo for alleged gender crimes in the Central African Republic, is set to begin in July 2010.

ICC prosecution efforts to date have been criticized for taking too much time to accomplish very little. Prosecutorial investigations, especially of those in senior leadership positions, have been impaired by insufficient expert capability. Where cases have been built, they have sometimes been quite small and of limited scope, with the high-profile charges against Sudanese president Omar al-Bashir the major exception. In numerous cases the ICC has also failed to secure the cooperation of states to arrest suspects. Internal management issues and difficulties in gathering evidence in war-torn and conflict-prone regions have also slowed the processing of cases and undercut the court's ability to begin more trials.

The fact that all cases have been brought against African defendants has also fueled criticism among African states that the ICC is biased. African states have criticized proceeding with the case against President Bashir, citing concerns about undermining peace efforts in Sudan. African critics have also complained about inadequate involvement of victims in the ICC's work, and insufficient expenditure of resources to improve the capacity of national courts to prosecute atrocity crimes.

Amid these problems, the primary U.S. concern—fear that a self-initiating prosecutor would zealously pursue cases counter to U.S. interests—has not materialized. The ICC rejected complaints against British soldiers in Iraq, who were alleged to have violated targeting rules and assisted in detainee abuse perpetrated by American forces. The ICC prosecutor did so because of the relatively small scale of the allegations, and because an ongoing British investigation of the allegations suggested the matter was being handled appropriately at the national level.

Nevertheless, concerns about the ICC in the United States remain, especially within the Pentagon and on Capitol Hill. National prosecutors in several European countries, including the United Kingdom, Italy, and Spain, have commenced investigations of U.S. officials and military personnel relating to military and intelligence actions in Iraq, Afghanistan, and in Europe itself, and critics allege regularly that civilian casualties from U.S. military operations amount to war crimes. These allegations heighten concerns in the Pentagon that the ICC might launch similar inquiries in the future. These concerns would be further exacerbated should the prosecutor open an investigation into war crimes allegedly committed by Israeli defense forces in Gaza during its 2008–2009 campaign.[8]

2010 Review Conference Agenda

The review conference is scheduled to convene in Kampala, Uganda, from May 31 to June 11, 2010. The conference will have two major components: consideration of proposed amendments to the Rome Statute and "stocktaking" on the performance of the ICC to date.

AGGRESSION

The most controversial item on the Kampala Review Conference agenda is whether to activate the ICC's jurisdiction over the crime of aggression. Two components comprise the international law of war: *jus ad bellum*, which regulates the decision to use force, and *jus in bello*, which regulates how force is used during armed conflicts. Violations of the latter are termed war crimes, and they have long been the subject of criminal prosecution. Aggression is a violation of the former, and its status within the pantheon of international crimes is less certain.

Both international military tribunals convened in Germany and Japan after World War II prosecuted "crimes against the peace," or aggression.[9] The United States supported prosecutions for crimes against the peace despite concerns raised by defense counsel and legal experts at the time that international law did not establish individual criminal liability for the conduct in question before World War II. Many scholars today therefore view those prosecutions as legally problematic.

Article 2(4) of the UN Charter sets out the current rule for the use of force: "All members shall refrain in their international relations from the threat or use of force against the territorial integrity or political independence of any state, or in any other manner inconsistent with the Purposes of the United Nations." The two exceptions to this rule recognized in the charter are self-defense and Chapter VII enforcement actions authorized by the Security Council. The charter entrusts the Security Council with authority to "determine the existence of . . . an act of aggression" and to take measures, including the use of force, in response to such a determination.

In 1974 the UN General Assembly adopted a draft definition of aggression for the purpose of clarifying for states when use of force ran afoul of international law. It defines aggression as "the use of armed force by a state against the sovereignty, territorial integrity or political independence of another state, or in any other manner inconsistent with the Charter of the United Nations, as set out in this Definition."[10] The General Assembly resolution contains a nonexhaustive list of acts that may constitute aggression, while leaving open the possibility that additional acts may constitute aggression as determined by the Security Council. The resolution represented a political compromise, and many international law experts believe this definition is too vague for the purposes of imposing individual criminal liability.

Given this history, it was not surprising that states were divided at Rome on whether to include aggression within the list of crimes under the jurisdiction of the ICC. Developing states and most European Union members supported including aggression; the United States and United Kingdom opposed it, at least absent an acceptable definition and preservation of the Security Council's primary role in this area. The final text of the Rome Statute included aggression within the jurisdiction of the ICC, but left for future amendment the definition of the crime and the conditions under which the ICC could proceed with a case. Thus, the ICC's jurisdiction over the crime of aggression has not yet been activated.

A Special Working Group on the Crime of Aggression ("Working Group") has proposed a draft definition of aggression for consideration at the review conference. The proposed amendment is notable in three respects. First, the same ambiguous definition of aggression used in the 1974 UN General Assembly resolution is proposed for use by the ICC. Second, only political and military leaders of states may perpetrate aggression; nonstate groups and rank-and-file members of the armed forces cannot. Third, jurisdiction is limited to an act of aggression, "which, by its character, gravity and scale, constitutes a manifest violation of the Charter of the United Nations." Although this term is designed to limit the ICC's jurisdiction to the most serious cases of aggression, "manifest" is not further defined.

Although the Working Group reached consensus on defining aggression, it could not agree on the circumstances or conditions under which the ICC may exercise jurisdiction over aggression. Two issues divided the Working Group. The first was whether the state whose nationals are alleged to have committed the crime must consent to the ICC's jurisdiction over aggression, or whether the consent of the victim state is sufficient. States in favor of requiring the consent of the alleged aggressor state argue that it is mandated by international law.[11] Opponents of this requirement fear it would undermine the ICC's ability to prosecute aggression.

Second, although the Working Group agreed that the ICC prosecutor was obligated to inform the Security Council of an intent to prosecute, it disagreed on whether the prosecutor could proceed absent Security Council authorization. The United Kingdom and France have argued that given the Security Council's primary role in regulating the use of force, including the determination that acts of aggression have occurred, it must have the last word on whether the ICC may move forward with prosecutions. Opponents of a decisive Security Council role have pointed to the risk of deadlock in the council, noting the council's historical reluctance to label actions as aggression. These states favor either allowing the prosecutor to proceed on his or her own accord absent Security Council action or providing the UN General Assembly or the International Court of Justice authority to conclude that an act of aggression has taken place, thereby activating ICC jurisdiction.

OPTIONS AND INTERESTS

Given these divisions, the review conference is faced with three options:

1. *Activate the ICC's aggression jurisdiction.* Doing so would require the review conference to adopt both a definition of aggression (either the Working Group's definition or a revised one) and agree on the conditions under which the ICC could proceed with a case, including the role of the Security Council. This would likely require a vote at the review conference, because no consensus currently exists on these issues.[12]

2. *Agree to a definition of aggression (either the Working Group's definition or a revised one), but send the issues relating to the conditions under*

which the ICC could proceed with cases to a new working group for further consideration. This may be the most likely scenario, given that several important state parties, including Japan, the United Kingdom, Australia, and Canada, have expressed opposition to proceeding on aggression without consensus.

3. *Send the entire aggression issue to a new working group for further consideration.* The United States is the only country to have openly advocated for this approach.

The top priority for the United States at the review conference should be to avoid amendment of the Rome Statute to activate jurisdiction over aggression. The lack of clear legal standards defining aggression poses dangers to the court's ability to function effectively and to U.S. security interests.

Unlike atrocity crimes, for which the content of international law is reasonably well established, the law on resort to force is more nebulous. The proposed definition reflects this uncertain state of the law by merely listing acts that might constitute aggression without defining when those acts are unlawful. The definition does not address how claims of self-defense or humanitarian necessity affect the categorization of the use of force as aggression. It is unclear, for example, whether NATO's 1999 Kosovo intervention would be criminal under the Working Group definition.

It is similarly unclear whether a preventive or preemptive strike against a proliferator of weapons of mass destruction (WMD)—for example, a U.S. or Israeli strike against suspected Iranian nuclear weapon program sites—would constitute criminal aggression. If the ICC claimed jurisdiction over such an attack, the ICC prosecutor and the ICC would have authority, but no clear guidance in the Rome Statute, to determine whether U.S. or Israeli action was an act of aggression or justified as an action in self-defense.[13]

A vague definition of aggression has practical consequences for the ICC. The court would be immediately entangled in international controversies regarding which side used force lawfully in an armed conflict. Had aggression jurisdiction been activated at Rome, the ICC might have been asked to decide whether the use of force was unlawful in controversial situations involving state parties, including French military intervention in Côte d'Ivoire in 2002 (France is a party), British and Polish invasion of Iraq in 2003 (United Kingdom and Poland are parties), and Russia's military incursion into Georgia in 2008 (Georgia is a party). Even where the states involved in a use of force are not parties to the Rome Statute, an alleged victim of aggression may consent to the ICC's jurisdiction after the use of force. If aggression existed as a crime in 2003, for example, Iraq could have consented to the jurisdiction of the ICC after the U.S. invasion, potentially exposing U.S. leaders to investigation and prosecution for the decision to use force. In such a scenario, the ICC prosecutor could have investigated U.S. or coalition partners, asking them for detailed explanations of their legal rationale as well as for classified intelligence information regarding Iraq's alleged weapons programs. The prosecutor might have then second-guessed the conclusion by the United States and other governments that their use of force was justified under existing UN Security Council resolutions.

Defining aggression vaguely could also have far-reaching security consequences even if the definition could not be applied to the United States without U.S. consent. For example, the lack of certainty could dissuade some potential coalition partners from participating in legitimate and important security or humanitarian operations because of the risk that their political leaders would subsequently be investigated by the ICC.

Even if the definition were clear, allowing ICC aggression prosecutions to proceed without Security Council authorization could undermine Security Council efforts—including ongoing diplomacy—to restore peace and stability in conflicts, perhaps by sending conflicting signals to the parties regarding the merits of the underlying dispute. In other cases, the prosecutor's decision not to investigate or prosecute aggression using his or her independent authority could be interpreted by the international community as legal acceptance, despite Security Council views to the contrary. These concerns suggest that the Security Council, which is entrusted by the UN Charter with responsibility for maintaining international peace and security, should oversee determinations regarding aggression.

These concerns are shared by all P5 states, including the United Kingdom and France, both parties to and strong supporters of the ICC. Many ICC advocates cherish the hope of eventual universality of membership, but an outcome on aggression that does not protect the prerogatives of the Security Council risks permanently pushing Russia and China, as well as the United States, away from the court. Although non-P5 states are less concerned about preserving Security Council authority, some recognize from a pragmatic standpoint the importance of support among P5 members for the court's agenda, given the practical difficulties in apprehending suspects and collecting evidence without the support of the most powerful states.

Activating aggression jurisdiction is also likely to exacerbate concerns about the ICC among U.S. interest groups and stakeholders, including on Capitol Hill and within the Pentagon. U.S. concerns about the ICC stem in part from the court's claim of the right to prosecute U.S. nationals without U.S. consent. Since the United States regularly deploys force in its role as a global superpower, it is substantially at risk of politicized second-guessing of the use of force by other states. This risk would be especially acute with regard to aggression jurisdiction because U.S. law does not criminalize acts of aggression. The United States cannot request an ICC prosecutor to defer to a U.S. domestic investigation of aggression, and Congress is highly unlikely to try to criminalize aggression by U.S. officials.[14]

Adding the crime of aggression to the ICC's responsibilities risks radically altering the way decisions to use force are regulated internationally in ways that harm the ICC, the international community, and the United States.

STOCKTAKING AND OTHER ITEMS

STOCKTAKING

The other major component of the review conference is "stocktaking," a critical evaluation of the performance of the ICC and state parties to the Rome Statute. Stocktaking represents an opportunity for the United States to use its experience in international justice to improve the function of the ICC and other international justice mechanisms. The value that the United States adds to this exercise will be a tangible demonstration of benefits to the ICC of American cooperation.

The stocktaking process will be divided into four half-day sessions:

– Victims Outreach: Limited outreach to victims' communities has reduced the impact of the ad hoc international criminal tribunals. This session will focus on how the ICC can enhance its impact in victims' communities, including through education and greater victim participation in trials.

- State Cooperation with the ICC: State parties are expected to cooperate with the ICC on a range of matters, including apprehension of suspects, evidence sharing, assistance in executing sentences, and financial contributions for maintenance of the court. This session will evaluate how to improve state cooperation.

- National Prosecution Capacity: A core premise of the ICC is that its jurisdiction arises only where national jurisdictions are unable or unwilling to prosecute. African states are concerned that the ICC has not provided the technical and financial assistance required to improve the capacity of national courts to handle prosecutions of serious crimes. This session will focus on how the ICC and other states may actively support national jurisdictions in capacity building.

- Peace and Justice: African states have raised concerns about the compatibility of ICC prosecutions with efforts to establish a lasting peace in societies emerging from conflict. This session intends to identify principles to guide efforts to seek international justice in areas with ongoing hostilities.

OTHER ITEMS

In addition to aggression and stocktaking, three other items are scheduled for consideration at the review conference. First, the review conference will consider a resolution calling on states and regional organizations to consider cooperation with the ICC through designation of facilities for housing ICC convicts. The goal of this resolution is to encourage a geographically broader grouping of states to make prisons available.

Second, the review conference will consider whether to continue to allow states the right to opt out of the war crimes jurisdiction of the ICC for its nationals for seven years after the state ratifies the statute. Colombia and France are the only parties that have availed themselves of this option.

Third, the review conference will consider an amendment to the Rome Statute to criminalize "employing poison or poisoned weapons; employing asphyxiating, poisonous or other gases, and all analogous liquids, materials or devices; and employing bullets which expand or flatten easily in the human body, which does not entirely cover the core or is pierced with incisions" in noninternational armed conflicts. The ICC currently has jurisdiction over the same crimes in international armed conflicts.

Recommendations

The United States should not seek to become a member of the ICC in the near term. When President Clinton authorized U.S. signature of the Rome Statute in 2000, he stated that he would not recommend that his successor transmit the treaty to the Senate until U.S. concerns had been addressed. These concerns included then, and include now, the heightened risk to the United States of politicized prosecutions and the lack of sufficient checks on the prosecutor's power. Although the ICC has not sought to prosecute any U.S. or allied official during its seven years in operation, the increasing willingness of foreign national prosecutors to investigate and prosecute U.S. officials and military personnel for actions in Iraq, Afghanistan, and elsewhere intensifies concerns that the ICC may wade into similar debates in the future. As a superpower with global responsibilities and legally exposed military forces deployed throughout the world, and as a permanent UN Security Council member with an interest in preserving that body's primary responsibility for ensuring peace and security, the United States therefore should not for the foreseeable future retreat from its past objections and seek to become a party to the Rome Statute. Even if the Obama administration or a successor administration were to submit the Rome Statute to the Senate for approval, the Senate would not approve it unless the treaty is amended or U.S. concerns are addressed in some other way.

That said, the United States should continue to build a cooperative relationship with the ICC unless state parties make major decisions in Kampala that undercut U.S. interests. The United States must act quickly, though, to solidify its negotiating position and make its case before the review conference. It should immediately undertake the following steps.

The United States should send a cabinet-level representative to Kampala to emphasize the cooperation between the United States and the ICC in ending impunity for perpetrators of atrocity crimes.

The review conference will begin with a plenary session in which representatives of state parties and observer states will have the opportunity to speak. Most states will be represented by ministerial-level officials. The Obama administration should send the secretary of state or national security adviser to provide an official statement on the relationship between the United States and the ICC. The mere presence of a cabinet-level representative will generate goodwill among the state parties while emphasizing the seriousness of U.S. concerns.

A statement superseding the 2002 Bush administration statement that broke off formal relations provides an opportunity to highlight the improved U.S. relationship with the ICC and the significant past and potential U.S. contribution to international justice. Clarity about the role the United States envisions for the ICC in prosecuting atrocity crimes also increases the legitimacy of U.S. arguments against activating aggression jurisdiction. The statement should include

- support for Security Council referral of atrocity crimes to the ICC, including standards the United States may apply in making this determination;
- commitment to support ICC investigations and prosecutions of atrocity crimes, in appropriate cases and where consistent with U.S. law;
- offer of assistance with development of ICC oversight capacities, consistent with U.S. law;
- commitment not to interfere with the decisions of states to become parties to the ICC; and
- openness to consideration of other mechanisms to formalize U.S.-ICC cooperation.

The United States should prepare a report describing its experience in all four stocktaking areas.

Stocktaking gives the United States an opportunity to provide constructive input on the ICC's current operational shortcomings. Most state parties want constructive evaluation of ICC performance. Responsive and helpful U.S. input in this task could improve the ICC, and it could also increase U.S. influence on the aggression debate. Encouraging a full and frank discussion of the current operational challenges facing the court may help persuade state parties that it is inappropriate to add aggression to the burden of the court.

The United States is well situated to provide input on all stocktaking sessions because of its traditional preeminent role in constructing and supporting international justice mechanisms. A U.S. report will improve the quality of the discussion in the stocktaking sessions, thereby increasing the likelihood of meaningful outputs emerging from Kampala. This report should cover several items:

– *Highlight lessons learned from past U.S. efforts to cooperate with international criminal tribunals.* Many states are concerned about the practical difficulties of cooperation with the ICC. U.S. cooperation with ad hoc tribunals, especially the International Criminal Tribunal for Yugoslavia (ICTY) and the International Criminal Tribunal for Rwanda (ICTR), positions the United States to provide advice on issues as diverse as sharing national security information with an international institution to working with local authorities to apprehend war crimes suspects.

– *Emphasize U.S. efforts to improve the capacity of national courts to prosecute serious crimes, especially in Africa.* African states are especially concerned that the ICC is failing to provide adequate capacity-building support to national courts to prosecute crimes within the ICC's jurisdiction. European states, by contrast, are reluctant to embrace a capacity-building role for the ICC, given an already overstretched court. The United States should highlight the full range of U.S.-sponsored legal capacity-building projects, to demonstrate commitment to national prosecutions of atrocity crimes and to emphasize the continuing need to support such efforts as part of an overall international justice strategy.

– *Respond to concerns of African states regarding the impact on peace posed by international justice efforts.* African states are concerned about the effect of ICC indictments on securing peace in the DRC and Sudan. The United States has particular experience working to balance peace and justice concerns from its involvement in ending fighting in the former Yugoslavia. The successes and failures encountered in resolving the conflict in the former Yugoslavia, while prosecuting those responsible for mass atrocities, provide useful lessons for future conflicts.

– *Provide guidance on domestic efforts in the United States to recognize the importance of a victim's concerns in the justice process.* African states are especially concerned with how to maximize the positive impact of international trials on victim groups, a legitimate concern given the poor performance of the ad hoc tribunals on this front. Victim groups in the United States are among the best organized in the world. U.S. experience in integrating victims' concerns into domestic justice procedures may provide useful insight on improving outreach from international tribunals.

The United States should push to avoid activation of the ICC's jurisdiction over the crime of aggression through a combination of strong red lines and flexible diplomacy.

A primary U.S. objective must be to avoid the activation of the crime of aggression, which is contrary to the interests of both the ICC and the United States. There are a range of possible outcomes that would satisfy core U.S. concerns, and U.S. negotiators will need to adjust their tactics accordingly as discussions unfold.

Much of the U.S. diplomatic outreach in advance of Kampala is best targeted at capitals and at the political level, where some of the concerns laid out above may receive greater consideration. For example, officials in capitals who regularly work with senior U.S. diplomats to manage security crises may be more sympathetic to security concerns than foreign officials who focus on international legal issues, and who typically make up foreign delegations to ICC discussions. Early initiation of the targeted diplomatic overtures suggested below, especially to NATO allies and influential regional powers such as Brazil and South Africa, is critical to laying the foundation for a successful review conference outcome. The White House should be prepared to supplement efforts by U.S. diplomats in outreach to capitals.

The United States should also work with states, such as the United Kingdom and France, that share common interests on aggression, rather than stand out in front of them. The goodwill created by the Obama administration's decision to participate at the review conference could be quickly dissipated by an overly assertive American strategy, especially if critics successfully characterize the United States as obstructionist. U.S. negotiators should avoid, in particular, turning the issue of aggression into a referendum on whether other countries want the future support of the United States.

Discussion of the aggression issue at Kampala is likely to proceed in a three-part sequence: (1) consideration of the Working Group definition of aggression, (2) determination of whether a state must consent before its nationals are subject to investigation and prosecution for aggression, and (3) decision on whether the Security Council makes the definitive determination on whether prosecutions for aggression may proceed.

The United States should emphasize at the outset its concerns about the proposed Working Group definition, which is vague in ways that risk miring the court in politicized investigations and fails to meet the basic international legal principle of clarity to ensure fairness for defendants. Even adopting this definition without activating aggression jurisdiction could be damaging, because individual states or other international courts might rely on it in ways that contribute to problematic legal precedent.

Although U.S. negotiators could suggest specific changes to the text that would improve its viability as a criminal provision, this strategy is unlikely to succeed and could be counterproductive. The Working Group achieved consensus on the definition, creating a sense among state parties that the issue is closed. The absence of the United States from the negotiating sessions of the Working Group will prompt many states to react negatively to even well-meaning definitional proposals at this stage. Offering alternative language may also create false expectations regarding U.S. support for aggression with an improved definition. Instead, clarity about U.S. concerns is likely the most effective way to convince state parties that further thought should be given to whether this definition advances the interests of international justice.

Should the review conference adopt the definition of aggression proposed by the Working Group, U.S. efforts should shift toward emphasizing the lack of consensus that exists about the conditions under which aggression jurisdiction should be activated. Many state parties, including Australia, Canada, Japan, and the United Kingdom, are wary of radically amending the Rome Statute without overwhelming or even unanimous consensus. Such consensus does not currently exist with respect to aggression. Rome Statute parties are evenly divided on the question of whether the consent of the alleged aggressor state is required to activate aggression jurisdiction. And although most states oppose limiting the ICC's jurisdiction over aggression to cases referred by the Security Council, there is no consensus on what alternative limits, if any, should be placed on the prosecutor's discretion to proceed with a case.

However, some Latin American and African states view consensus as less important than activating aggression jurisdiction, and they may push for votes at the review conference on contentious issues. Should this occur, the United States must be clear that it will not support an outcome that allows the prosecutor to proceed with aggression prosecutions absent the consent of both parties involved and approval of the Security Council.

On consent, the United States should stand with states arguing that consent of the aggressor state is required under international law as a prerequisite to ICC jurisdiction. A consent requirement protects significant U.S. interests by ensuring that no U.S. (or allied) personnel will be prosecuted for aggression without the consent of the United States (or ally).

As for the role of the Security Council, arguments to preserve the legal prerogatives of the Security Council in this area should acknowledge the organization's past shortcomings in responding to allegations of aggression. Nevertheless, given the inherently political nature of evaluating the use of force and the need to consider designations of aggression in the context of broader efforts to resolve conflicts and preserve stability, there is no viable substitute for Security Council primacy in making aggression determinations. P5 efforts should emphasize that jurisdiction over aggression will be most effective with assistance from the Security Council, which is ensured when the council refers the case. Emphasis should also be placed on the risks to the ICC's legitimacy in conducting atrocity crimes prosecutions if the court is viewed as politicized on account of its involvement with aggression.

The United States should make clear that if the state parties decide to activate the court's jurisdiction over aggression without consensus (and by implication without addressing the most significant U.S. concerns), the likelihood that important nonparty states, including the United States, Russia, and China, will join the court will be greatly diminished. Activating the court's jurisdiction over aggression also makes it harder for the United States to cooperate with the court, even as a nonparty. This is not intended as a negotiating threat but as a statement of strategic and political realities.

The United States should avoid obstructing the decisions of state parties on items of the review conference agenda where the United States lacks a national interest.

Given the need for the United States to be active on the issue of aggression, and the opportunity to participate constructively in the stock-taking sessions, the delegation should remain neutral, or even voice support, on the remaining agenda items if they do not implicate significant U.S. interests. The United States should, for example, defer to state parties on the call for a greater number of facilities to house ICC convicts. Widespread support exists for this resolution, and if and when the ICC does convict and sentence defendants, it will need adequate facilities to house prisoners. The United States should also defer to state parties on the repeal of the seven-year opt-out provision. There is a division among state parties between those who wish to repeal the provision as an affront to the purposes of the Rome Statute and those who see no reason to tinker with a rarely used provision. Because the United States is unlikely to use such a provision, it should remain on the sidelines on this issue.

In preparing for Kampala the U.S. government should determine whether it has national security concerns about expanding the criminal prohibition of the use of various weapons to noninternational armed conflict. The United States is currently engaged in a noninternational armed conflict with al-Qaeda. Extending any criminal prohibition from international to noninternational armed conflict must be assessed in light of current and anticipated military practices and existing treaty commitments on weapons use. The Department of Defense will be best positioned to determine whether this proposal is consistent with U.S. interests and operational requirements.

If U.S. objectives are achieved at Kampala, the United States should consider steps to expand cooperation with the ICC.

The United States has security and moral interests in ensuring that those responsible for atrocity crimes be held accountable, and the ICC can be an important tool to achieve these goals. With so many states now party to the ICC, the reality is that the ICC will be the presumptive forum for future international trials. It is unlikely that state parties would support creating new ad hoc tribunals like those for Yugoslavia, Rwanda, Sierra Leone, or other cases that predated the ICC.

At some future point, if U.S. concerns could be addressed through changes to the court, it would be desirable for the United States to become a member. As a global superpower, the United States would gain direct and substantial influence over the court and its work, including the selection of ICC judges and prosecutors. The prosecutors set the agenda for the ICC, which is important to the United States because of the court's potential contribution to the stability of conflict zones through reestablishment of the rule of law. The judges develop and interpret international human rights law and the law of war in ways that could affect U.S. and allied military operations abroad. Putting the full weight of U.S. power and influence behind the court's work would make it a powerful institution for combating impunity of mass atrocity perpetrators.

But absent significant changes to the ICC, U.S. membership remains unlikely for the foreseeable future. The increased scrutiny of, and legal challenges to, the actions of U.S. and coalition military forces in recent years is likely to deepen concerns about the impact the ICC could have on U.S. interests. Moreover, the Senate, which would be required to approve the Rome Statute by a two-thirds vote, has been highly skeptical of multilateral treaties seen as impinging upon U.S. sovereignty; the Senate would certainly not consent to the Rome Statute in its current form, and may never be willing to approve the treaty. Moreover, the ICC has failed to accumulate a record of accomplishment to date that could be used to overcome political resistance.

If U.S. objectives are achieved at Kampala, however, the United States could take a range of practical steps short of membership to improve the ICC's ability to conduct investigations, apprehend suspects, and complete successful prosecutions. These steps include training and funding investigators and prosecutors, providing political and military assistance to apprehend suspects, sharing intelligence and other evidence to aid case development, and giving assistance in developing an oversight mechanism. Providing some of this assistance, though, would require repeal of all or parts of ASPA, which would be politically difficult for the Obama administration.

The United States could also formalize its relationship as a "non-party partner" of the court. Assuming legal restrictions in ASPA could be addressed, the United States could commit to make available to the court significant resources vital to its effective operation. For their part, the ICC and its state parties would recognize that the global security responsibilities of its U.S. partner raise unique or heightened concerns with the court that call for careful discretion when U.S. interests or nationals are directly involved. Such recognition is difficult to square with universality, a principle at the heart of the international justice agenda, but would open the door to effective collaboration between the ICC and the United States in combating the worst atrocity crimes.

CONCLUSION: KAMPALA AND BEYOND

The ICC and its relationship with the United States are at a crossroads. Although the United States is unlikely to join the court any time soon, the outcome in Kampala will help define the U.S. position toward the court for many years to come. If U.S. efforts are successful, opportunities exist to further strengthen cooperation with the court and its state parties that promote international justice while protecting U.S. interests.

Endnotes

1. Recent studies have suggested steps the United States can take to improve cooperation with the ICC. See Lee Feinstein and Tod Lindberg, *Means to an End: U.S. Inter-
   est in the International Criminal Court* (Washington, DC: Brookings Institution Press,
   2009); Report of an American Society of International Law independent task force,
   U.S. Policy Toward the International Criminal Court: Furthering Positive Engagement
   (Washington, DC: American Society of International Law, 2009); David Scheffer and
   John Hutson, *Strategy for U.S. Engagement with the International Criminal Court* (New
   York: The Century Foundation, 2008). This report is focused on the more specific task
   of how the United States should approach the review conference and the effect of the
   review conference on its relationship with the ICC for years to come.
2. States joining the United States in voting against the text at Rome were China, Israel,
   Iraq, Libya, Qatar, and Yemen.
3. In *proprio motu* prosecutions, in order to proceed the prosecutor must receive approval of the Pre-Trial Chamber, which is composed of judges with criminal trial experience. Rome Statute of the International Criminal Court, Article 15(3)-(4).
4. State Department press release: "International Criminal Court: Letter to UN Secre-
   tary-General Kofi Annan," May 6, 2002 (Appendix C).
5. Marc Grossman, former U.S. undersecretary of state, "American Foreign Policy
   and the International Criminal Court," speech delivered at the Center for International Strategic Studies, May 6, 2002, http://www.coalitionfortheicc.org/documents/
   USUnsigningGrossman6May02.pdf.
6. See, for example, John B. Bellinger III, former U.S. Department of State legal adviser,
   "The United States and the International Criminal Court: Where We've Been and
   Where We're Going," speech delivered at DePaul University College of Law, April 25,
   2008, and John B. Bellinger III, "The United States and International Law," speech
   delivered at The Hague, Netherlands, June 6, 2007.
7. State Department spokesperson Ian Kelly explained, "We will participate in these
   meetings as an observer and there will be an interagency delegation comprising of State
   Department and Defense department officials, which will allow us to advance, use and
   engage all the delegations in various matters of interest to the U.S., specifically, our concerns about the definition of a crime of aggression, which is one of the main topics for
   discussion at this conference. This in no way suggests that we have—we don't—we no
   longer have concerns about the ICC. We do have concerns about it. We have specific
   concerns about assertion of jurisdiction over nationals of a nonparty state and the ability to exercise that jurisdiction without authorizations by the Security Council." Ian
   Kelly, U.S. Department of State spokesperson, press briefing remarks delivered November 16, 2009, http://www.state.gov/r/pa/prs/dpb/2009/nov/131982.htm.
8. Israel is not a state party, and the Palestinian Authority is not a recognized state, raising
   serious questions about whether the ICC can investigate the claims consistent with the

Rome Statute. Article 12(3) of the Rome Statute allows states that are not parties to the statute to accept the jurisdiction of the ICC with respect to a particular crime. While the Palestinian Authority has filed such a declaration covering crimes committed in Gaza, it is unclear whether it can do so because it is not a recognized state. A decision by the prosecutor to allow the case to proceed would suggest willingness to read the Rome Statute's jurisdictional grant broadly.

9.   The IMT Statute for Nuremberg defined crimes against the peace as "planning, preparation, initiation, or waging of a war of aggression, or a war in violation of international treaties, agreements or assurances, or participation in a common plan or conspiracy to achieve any of the foregoing."

10. Resolution 3314 makes two changes to Article 2(4) of the UN Charter. First, it replaces "threat or use of force" with "armed force," suggesting mere threats do not amount to aggression. Second, it adds the term "sovereignty," not found in Article 2(4). United Nations General Assembly Resolution 3314 (XXIX). Annex. UN Doc. A/RES/3314 (December 14, 1974).

11. The jurisdiction of the ICC in cases where a crime is committed by nationals of non-parties in the territory of a state party is derived from the party's right under international law to prosecute crimes that occur in its territory. If the crime of aggression takes place solely in the territory of the aggressor state, there would be no basis to proceed with claims against the aggressor state's nationals without its consent. Additionally, Article 121(5) of the Rome Statute limits application of amendments to state parties' nationals who have consented to the amendment, meaning aggression prosecutions cannot proceed against a state party's nationals without its prior consent to the court's jurisdiction over aggression.

12. Article 121(3) of the Rome Statute allows for adoption of amendments at a review conference with a majority of two-thirds of state parties where consensus cannot be reached. Under Article 121(5), if the amendment is to the substantive offenses of the Rome Statute, the amendment goes into effect for state parties that accept the amendment one year after ratification. The court will not assume jurisdiction over nationals of state parties that have not ratified the amendment. Article 121(4) provides that other amendments to the Rome Statute go into force once seven-eighths of states have ratified the amendment.

13. This assumes that ICC parties had not agreed to require the consent of both parties for investigation of alleged acts of aggression.

14. Any attempt to do so would raise serious constitutional questions about whether the judiciary could adjudicate the legality of the decision to use force consistent with separation of powers.

About the Author

Vijay Padmanabhan is a visiting assistant professor of law at Yeshiva University's Benjamin N. Cardozo School of Law. Professor Padmanabhan teaches the law of war and human rights law, and has published on topics in international criminal law and international humanitarian law. From 2003 to 2008, he was an attorney-adviser in the office of the legal adviser at the U.S. Department of State. While there he served as the department's chief counsel for law of war–related litigation, including collaborating with the U.S. Department of Justice on the Boumediene, Omar, and Hamdan cases in the U.S. Supreme Court. He also was the department liaison to the office of military commissions in the U.S. Department of Defense. Padmanabhan was a law clerk to the Honorable James L. Dennis of the U.S. Court of Appeals for the Fifth Circuit. He received his BSBA summa cum laude from Georgetown University and JD magna cum laude from New York University School of Law.

Advisory Committee for
From Rome to Kampala

John B. Bellinger III, *Project Director,*
ex officio
Council on Foreign Relations

Matthew C. Waxman, *Project Director,*
ex officio
Council on Foreign Relations

Elliott Abrams, *ex officio*
Council on Foreign Relations

Kenneth Anderson
American University

Gary J. Bass
Princeton University

Kenneth J. Bialkin
Skadden, Arps, Slate, Meagher & Flom LLP

David M. Crane
Syracuse University

Daniel J. Dell'Orto
AM General LLC

Richard Dicker
Human Rights Watch

Mark A. Drumbl
Washington & Lee University School of Law

Richard H. Fontaine Jr.
Center for a New American Security

Michael J. Glennon
The Fletcher School of Law & Diplomacy,
Tufts University

Marc Grossman
The Cohen Group

Larry D. Johnson
Columbia University School of Law

David A. Kaye
University of California, Los Angeles

Neil Kritz
U.S. Institute of Peace

Tod Lindberg
Hoover Institution, Stanford University

Troland S. Link
Davis Polk & Wardwell LLP

Michael J. Matheson
George Washington University Law School

Judith A. Miller

Sean D. Murphy
George Washington University Law School

Michael A. Newton
Vanderbilt Law School

Stewart M. Patrick, *ex officio*
Council on Foreign Relations

Pierre-Richard Prosper
Arent Fox PLLC

Stephen G. Rademaker
BGR Group

Kal Raustiala
University of California, Los Angeles

Stephen Rickard
Open Society Institute

Nicholas Rostow
State University of New York

Council Special Reports

Published by the Council on Foreign Relations

Strengthening the Nuclear Nonproliferation Regime
Paul Lettow; CSR No. 54, April 2010
An International Institutions and Global Governance Program Report

The Russian Economic Crisis
Jeffrey Mankoff; CSR No. 53, April 2010

Somalia: A New Approach
Bronwyn E. Bruton; CSR No. 52, March 2010
A Center for Preventive Action Report

The Future of NATO
James M. Goldgeier; CSR No. 51, February 2010
An International Institutions and Global Governance Program Report

The United States in the New Asia
Evan A. Feigenbaum and Robert A. Manning; CSR No. 50, November 2009
An International Institutions and Global Governance Program Report

Intervention to Stop Genocide and Mass Atrocities: International Norms and U.S. Policy
Matthew C. Waxman; CSR No. 49, October 2009
An International Institutions and Global Governance Program Report

Enhancing U.S. Preventive Action
Paul B. Stares and Micah Zenko; CSR No. 48, October 2009
A Center for Preventive Action Report

The Canadian Oil Sands: Energy Security vs. Climate Change
Michael A. Levi; CSR No. 47, May 2009
A Maurice R. Greenberg Center for Geoeconomic Studies Report

The National Interest and the Law of the Sea
Scott G. Borgerson; CSR No. 46, May 2009

Lessons of the Financial Crisis
Benn Steil; CSR No. 45, March 2009
A Maurice R. Greenberg Center for Geoeconomic Studies Report

Global Imbalances and the Financial Crisis
Steven Dunaway; CSR No. 44, March 2009
A Maurice R. Greenberg Center for Geoeconomic Studies Report

Eurasian Energy Security
Jeffrey Mankoff; CSR No. 43, February 2009

Preparing for Sudden Change in North Korea
Paul B. Stares and Joel S. Wit; CSR No. 42, January 2009
A Center for Preventive Action Report

Averting Crisis in Ukraine
Steven Pifer; CSR No. 41, January 2009
A Center for Preventive Action Report

Congo: Securing Peace, Sustaining Progress
Anthony W. Gambino; CSR No. 40, October 2008
A Center for Preventive Action Report

Deterring State Sponsorship of Nuclear Terrorism
Michael A. Levi; CSR No. 39, September 2008

China, Space Weapons, and U.S. Security
Bruce W. MacDonald; CSR No. 38, September 2008

Sovereign Wealth and Sovereign Power: The Strategic Consequences of American Indebtedness
Brad W. Setser; CSR No. 37, September 2008
A Maurice R. Greenberg Center for Geoeconomic Studies Report

Securing Pakistan's Tribal Belt
Daniel Markey; CSR No. 36, July 2008 (Web-only release) and August 2008
A Center for Preventive Action Report

Avoiding Transfers to Torture
Ashley S. Deeks; CSR No. 35, June 2008

Global FDI Policy: Correcting a Protectionist Drift
David M. Marchick and Matthew J. Slaughter; CSR No. 34, June 2008
A Maurice R. Greenberg Center for Geoeconomic Studies Report

Dealing with Damascus: Seeking a Greater Return on U.S.-Syria Relations
Mona Yacoubian and Scott Lasensky; CSR No. 33, June 2008
A Center for Preventive Action Report

Climate Change and National Security: An Agenda for Action
Joshua W. Busby; CSR No. 32, November 2007
A Maurice R. Greenberg Center for Geoeconomic Studies Report

Planning for Post-Mugabe Zimbabwe
Michelle D. Gavin; CSR No. 31, October 2007
A Center for Preventive Action Report

The Case for Wage Insurance
Robert J. LaLonde; CSR No. 30, September 2007
A Maurice R. Greenberg Center for Geoeconomic Studies Report

Reform of the International Monetary Fund
Peter B. Kenen; CSR No. 29, May 2007
A Maurice R. Greenberg Center for Geoeconomic Studies Report

Nuclear Energy: Balancing Benefits and Risks
Charles D. Ferguson; CSR No. 28, April 2007

Nigeria: Elections and Continuing Challenges
Robert I. Rotberg; CSR No. 27, April 2007
A Center for Preventive Action Report

The Economic Logic of Illegal Immigration
Gordon H. Hanson; CSR No. 26, April 2007
A Maurice R. Greenberg Center for Geoeconomic Studies Report

The United States and the WTO Dispute Settlement System
Robert Z. Lawrence; CSR No. 25, March 2007
A Maurice R. Greenberg Center for Geoeconomic Studies Report

Bolivia on the Brink
Eduardo A. Gamarra; CSR No. 24, February 2007
A Center for Preventive Action Report

After the Surge: The Case for U.S. Military Disengagement from Iraq
Steven N. Simon; CSR No. 23, February 2007

Darfur and Beyond: What Is Needed to Prevent Mass Atrocities
Lee Feinstein; CSR No. 22, January 2007

Avoiding Conflict in the Horn of Africa: U.S. Policy Toward Ethiopia and Eritrea
Terrence Lyons; CSR No. 21, December 2006
A Center for Preventive Action Report

Living with Hugo: U.S. Policy Toward Hugo Chávez's Venezuela
Richard Lapper; CSR No. 20, November 2006
A Center for Preventive Action Report

Reforming U.S. Patent Policy: Getting the Incentives Right
Keith E. Maskus; CSR No. 19, November 2006
A Maurice R. Greenberg Center for Geoeconomic Studies Report

Foreign Investment and National Security: Getting the Balance Right
Alan P. Larson and David M. Marchick; CSR No. 18, July 2006
A Maurice R. Greenberg Center for Geoeconomic Studies Report

Challenges for a Postelection Mexico: Issues for U.S. Policy
Pamela K. Starr; CSR No. 17, June 2006 (Web-only release) and November 2006

U.S.-India Nuclear Cooperation: A Strategy for Moving Forward
Michael A. Levi and Charles D. Ferguson; CSR No. 16, June 2006

Generating Momentum for a New Era in U.S.-Turkey Relations
Steven A. Cook and Elizabeth Sherwood-Randall; CSR No. 15, June 2006

Peace in Papua: Widening a Window of Opportunity
Blair A. King; CSR No. 14, March 2006
A Center for Preventive Action Report

Neglected Defense: Mobilizing the Private Sector to Support Homeland Security
Stephen E. Flynn and Daniel B. Prieto; CSR No. 13, March 2006

Afghanistan's Uncertain Transition From Turmoil to Normalcy
Barnett R. Rubin; CSR No. 12, March 2006
A Center for Preventive Action Report

Preventing Catastrophic Nuclear Terrorism
Charles D. Ferguson; CSR No. 11, March 2006

Getting Serious About the Twin Deficits
Menzie D. Chinn; CSR No. 10, September 2005
A Maurice R. Greenberg Center for Geoeconomic Studies Report

Both Sides of the Aisle: A Call for Bipartisan Foreign Policy
Nancy E. Roman; CSR No. 9, September 2005

Forgotten Intervention? What the United States Needs to Do in the Western Balkans
Amelia Branczik and William L. Nash; CSR No. 8, June 2005
A Center for Preventive Action Report

A New Beginning: Strategies for a More Fruitful Dialogue with the Muslim World
Craig Charney and Nicole Yakatan; CSR No. 7, May 2005

Power-Sharing in Iraq
David L. Phillips; CSR No. 6, April 2005
A Center for Preventive Action Report

Giving Meaning to "Never Again": Seeking an Effective Response to the Crisis in Darfur and Beyond
Cheryl O. Igiri and Princeton N. Lyman; CSR No. 5, September 2004

Freedom, Prosperity, and Security: The G8 Partnership with Africa: Sea Island 2004 and Beyond
J. Brian Atwood, Robert S. Browne, and Princeton N. Lyman; CSR No. 4, May 2004

Addressing the HIV/AIDS Pandemic: A U.S. Global AIDS Strategy for the Long Term
Daniel M. Fox and Princeton N. Lyman; CSR No. 3, May 2004
Cosponsored with the Milbank Memorial Fund

Challenges for a Post-Election Philippines
Catharin E. Dalpino; CSR No. 2, May 2004
A Center for Preventive Action Report

Stability, Security, and Sovereignty in the Republic of Georgia
David L. Phillips; CSR No. 1, January 2004
A Center for Preventive Action Report

To purchase a printed copy, call the Brookings Institution Press: 800.537.5487.
Note: Council Special Reports are available for download from CFR's website, www.cfr.org.
For more information, email publications@cfr.org.